"THE BASICS"
What You Need To Know About Teen Dating Violence (TDV)

Kesha Stowe-Spence

DEDICATION

This book is dedicated to the youth, today's generation, tomorrow's generation and future generations to come. Know that you and only you should hold the power to your own happiness.

~Air Hugs~

CONTENTS

THE REALITY OF TEEN DATING VIOLENCE

Unhealthy relationship behaviors often start early and lead to a lifetime of abuse. Domestic violence does not only affect adults, it is now the reality of our youth. Every student, parent and teacher needs to be aware of teen dating violence. Each year one in five adolescents report being a victim of verbal or emotional abuse and unfortunately verbal and emotional abuse can be just as damaging as physical abuse, if not worst. As one wise person once said; tell a young lady she is beautiful she will believe it for a minute, tell a young lady she is worthless she will remember it for the rest of her life.

Many teen girls who have been in a relationship said that their boyfriends had threatened violence to them or self-harm in the event of a break-up. Unfortunately, these young women/men who have been victim of physical, verbal and emotional abuse; in their dating relationships continue to date the abusers.

Awareness and educating one's self and each other is the key in defeating this epidemic known as teen dating violence. Teen dating abuse does not only affect the victim and their abuser, it affects everyone around them including friends, families and communities.

Step Up, Speak Out, Love doesn't hurt!

1 UNDERSTANDING TEEN DATING VIOLENCE

KESHA STOWE-SPENCE

Dating violence is a pattern of controlling behaviors that one partner use to gain power over the other, and it includes:

☐ Any kind of physical violence or threat of physical violence to get control.

☐ Emotional or mental abuse, such as playing mind games, making you feel crazy, or constantly putting you down or criticizing you.

☐ Sexual abuse, including making you do anything you don't want to, refusing to have safe sex or making you feel badly about yourself sexually.

Does your boyfriend/girlfriend:

• Have a history of bad relationships or past violence; always blames his/her problems on other people; or blames you for "making" him/her treat you badly?

• Try to use drugs or alcohol to coerce you or get you alone when you don't want to be?

KESHA STOWE-SPENCE

• Try to control you by being bossy, not taking your opinion seriously or making all of the decisions about who you see, what you wear, what you do, etc.?

• Talk negatively about people in sexual ways or talk about sex like it's a game or contest?

Do you:

• Feel less confident about yourself when you're with him/her?

• Feel scared or worried about doing or saying "the wrong thing?"

• Find yourself changing your behavior out of fear or to avoid a fight.

Dating violence is more than just arguing or fighting.

Teens who abuse their girlfriends or boyfriends do the same things that adults who abuse their partners do. Teen dating violence is just as serious as adult domestic violence.

Teens are seriously at risk for dating

KESHA STOWE-SPENCE

violence. Research shows that physical or sexual abuse is a part of 1 in 3 high school relationships.

In 95% of abusive relationships, men abuse women; however young women can also be violent, and young men can be victims. Gay, lesbian, bisexual and trans-gendered teens are just as at risk for abuse in their relationships as anyone else.

Abusive relationships have good times and bad times. Part of what makes dating violence so confusing and painful is that there is love mixed with the abuse. This can make it hard to tell if you are really being abused.

Unfortunately, without help the violence will only get worse. If you think you may be in an abusive relationship, please call the **National Dating Abuse Helpline** to talk with someone about it. You can also call the Helpline for more information about dating violence or other resources for teens. The National Domestic Violence number is 1-800-799-SAFE.

KESHA STOWE-SPENCE

2 TEEN POWER & CONTROL WHEEL

KESHA STOWE-SPENCE

The **power and control wheel** was designed to teach victims the different types of abuse that falls under domestic violence. So many people are victims of domestic violence but they are not aware of it. Most believe that domestic violence is when a person uses a part of their body or object to cause harm to another but there are many other forms of domestic abuse. The **power and control wheel** teaches you the different types of abuse that fall under the categories of being a victim of teen dating abuse.

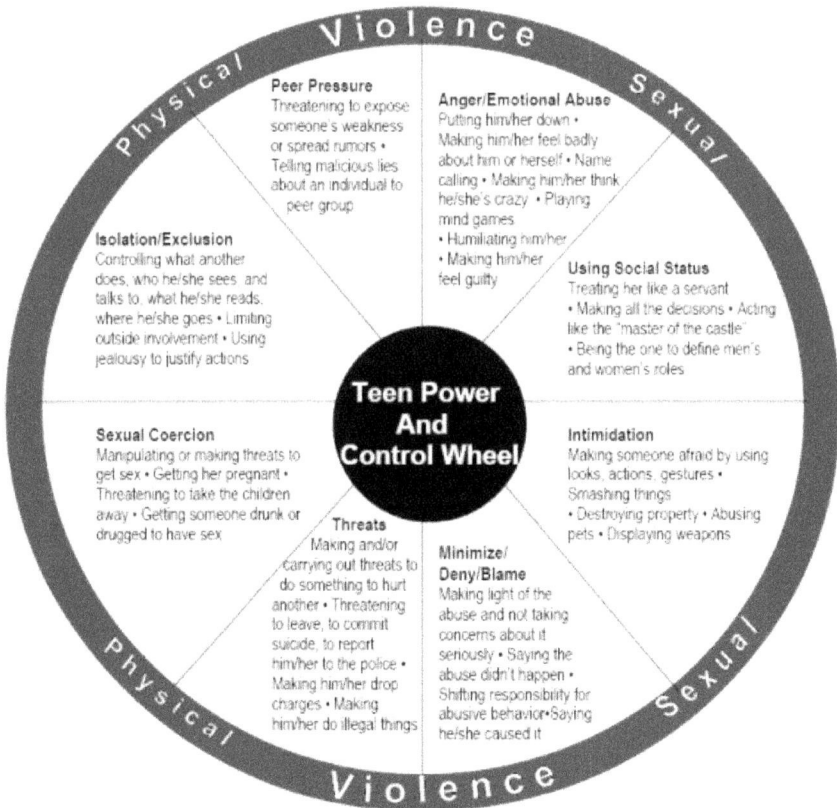

Violence

Physical

Sexual

Peer Pressure
Threatening to expose someone's weakness or spread rumors • Telling malicious lies about an individual to peer group

Anger/Emotional Abuse
Putting him/her down • Making him/her feel badly about him or herself • Name calling • Making him/her think he/she's crazy • Playing mind games • Humiliating him/her • Making him/her feel guilty

Isolation/Exclusion
Controlling what another does, who he/she sees and talks to, what he/she reads, where he/she goes • Limiting outside involvement • Using jealousy to justify actions

Using Social Status
Treating her like a servant • Making all the decisions • Acting like the "master of the castle" • Being the one to define men's and women's roles

Teen Power And Control Wheel

Sexual Coercion
Manipulating or making threats to get sex • Getting her pregnant • Threatening to take the children away • Getting someone drunk or drugged to have sex

Intimidation
Making someone afraid by using looks, actions, gestures • Smashing things • Destroying property • Abusing pets • Displaying weapons

Threats
Making and/or carrying out threats to do something to hurt another • Threatening to leave, to commit suicide, to report him/her to the police • Making him/her drop charges • Making him/her do illegal things

Minimize/ Deny/Blame
Making light of the abuse and not taking concerns about it seriously • Saying the abuse didn't happen • Shifting responsibility for abusive behavior•Saying he/she caused it

Physical

Sexual

Violence

11

Types of Abuse you'll find on the Power & Control Wheel

Anger/Emotional Abuse

Putting him/her down * Making him/her feel badly about him or herself * Name calling * Making him or her think he/she is crazy * Playing mind games * Humiliating him/her * Making him/her feel guilty

Using Social Status

Treating him/her like a servant * Making all the decisions * Acting like the master of the castle * Being the one to define men and women roles

Intimidation

Making someone afraid by using looks, actions, or gestures * Destroying property * Abusing pets * Displaying weapons

Minimize/Deny/Blame

Making light of the abuse and not taking concerns seriously * Saying the abuse did not happen * Shifting responsibility for abusive behavior * Saying he/she caused it

Threats

Making and/or carrying out threats to do something to hurt another * Threating to leave, to commit suicide to report him/her to the police * Making him/her drop charges * Making him/her do illegal things

Sexual Coercion

Manipulating or making threats to get sex * Getting her pregnant * Threatening to take the child/children away * Getting someone drunk or drugged to have sex

Isolation/Exclusion

Controlling what another does, who he/she sees, and talk to, what he or she reads, where he/she goes * Limiting outside involvement * Using jealousy to justify actions

Peer Pressure

Threating to expose someone's weakness or spread rumors * Telling malicious lies about an individual to a group of peer group

Cyber Abuse

Cyber Abuse is not on the power and control wheel but it is definitely a form of abuse *

KESHA STOWE-SPENCE

Texting offensive remarks about him/her * Sending inappropriate photos on social media through the Internet or cell phones

Learning and understanding the different types of abuse and not allowing one to treat you as such can help prevent you from being a victim of teen dating violence. Knowledge is Power!

3 WHY DO PEOPLE STAY IN ABUSIVE RELATIONSHIPS

People who have never been abused often wonder why victims just don't leave. They don't understand that breaking up can be more complicated than it seems. There are many reasons why both men and women stay in abusive relationships. If you have a friend in an unhealthy relationship, support them by trying to understand why they may choose to **not** leave immediately. Give that victim the time he/she needs to make the decision on his/her own.

Conflicting Emotions may be the reason:

☐ **Fear:** Your friend may be afraid of what will happen if they decide to leave the relationship. If their partner, family or friends have threatened your friend, they may not feel safe leaving.

☐ **Believing Abuse is Normal:** If your friend doesn't know what a healthy relationship looks like; perhaps from growing up in an environment where abuse was common, they may not recognize that their relationship is unhealthy.

KESHA STOWE-SPENCE

☐ **Fear of Being Exposed:** If your friend is in same-sex relationship and has not yet come out to everyone, his or her partner may threaten to reveal this secret. Being exposed may feel especially scary for young people who are just beginning to explore their sexuality.

☐ **Embarrassment:** It's probably hard for your friend to admit that they've been abused. They may feel they've done something wrong by becoming involved with an abusive partner. They may also worry that their friends and family will judge them.

☐ **Low Self-esteem:** If your friend's partner constantly puts them down and blames them for the abuse, it can be easy for your friend to believe those statements and think that the abuse is their fault.

☐ **Love:** Your friend may stay in an abusive relationship hoping that their abuser will change. Think about it—if a person you love tells you they'll change, you want to believe them. Your friend may only want the violence to stop, not for the relationship to end entirely.

Pressure:

☐ **Social/Peer Pressure:** If the abuser is popular, it can be hard for a person to tell their friends for fear that no one will believe them or that everyone will take the abuser's side.

☐ **Cultural/Religious Reasons:** Traditional gender roles can make it difficult for the abused. Also, your friend's culture or religion may influence them to stay, rather than end the relationship for fear or bringing shame upon the family.

Pregnancy/Parenting: Your friend may feel pressure to raise their children with both parents together, even if that means staying in an abusive relationship. Also, the abusive partner may threaten to take or harm the children if your friend leaves.

These are just a few reasons why many victims stay but believe me there are many more.

What Can You Do as a Friend?

If you have friends or family members who are in unhealthy or abusive relationships, the most important thing you can do and I cannot say it enough, is be supportive and listen to them. ***PLEASE DO NOT JUDGE!***

Understand that leaving an unhealthy or abusive relationship is ***NEVER*** easy. Try to let your friend know that they have options and there are many resources that are available.

4 HOW TO GET OUT

KESHA STOWE-SPENCE

As simple as it may seem to others it is not always that simple to get out of an unhealthy relationship. As victims we know this all to well. First and foremost you must learn to love you and love you unconditionally. To love yourself unconditionally will not let you accept anything but kindness when it comes to being in a relationship. If you are treated anyway other than that yourself love will not allow it.

Victims need to find someone they can talk to that will not pass judgment. We pretty much know the people that we have in our lives and if they are not able to show empathy that may not be the person to turn to.

I recommend talking to your parents first. If that does not help you can speak with your guidance counselor, an adult that you trust, or the authorities that are available and can get you the necessary help that is needed.

HOW TO HELP A FRIEND GET OUT

Don't be afraid to let him or her know that you are concerned for their safety. Help your friend or family member recognize the abuse. Tell him or her you see what is going on and that you want to help. Help them

recognize that what is happening is not "normal" and that they deserve a healthy, non-violent relationship.

Acknowledge that he or she is in a very difficult and scary situation. Let your friend or family member know that the abuse is not their fault. Reassure him or her that they are not alone and that there is help and support out there.

Be supportive. Listen to your friend or family member. Remember that it may be difficult for him or her to talk about the abuse. Let him or her know that you are available to help whenever they may need it. What they need most is someone who will believe and listen to them.

Be non-judgmental. Respect your friend or family member's decisions. There are many reasons why victims stay in abusive relationships. He or she may leave and return to the relationship many times. Do not criticize his or her decisions or try to guilt them. He or she will need your support even more during those times.

Encourage him or her to participate in activities outside of the relationship with friends and family.

If he or she ends the relationship, continue to be supportive of them. Even though the relationship was abusive, your friend or family member may still feel sad and lonely once it is over. He or she will need time to mourn the loss of the relationship and will especially need your support at that time.

Help him or her to develop a safety plan.

Encourage him or her to talk to people who can provide help and guidance. Find a local domestic violence agency that provides counseling or support groups. Offer to go with him or her to talk to family and friends. If he or she needs to go to the police station, court, or appointment with a lawyer, offer to go along for moral support.

Remember that you cannot "rescue" him or her. Although it is difficult to see someone you care about getting hurt, ultimately the person getting hurt has to be the one to decide that they want to do something about it. It's important for you to support him or her and help them find a way to safety and peace.

5 YOUR DATING BILL OF RIGHTS

YOUR DATING BILL OF RIGHTS...

YOU HAVE THE RIGHT:

To always be treated with respect.

YOU HAVE THE RIGHT:

To be in a healthy relationship.

YOU HAVE THE RIGHT:

To not be hurt physically or emotionally.

YOU HAVE THE RIGHT:

To refuse sex or affection at any time.

YOU HAVE THE RIGHT:

To have friends and activities apart from your significant other.

YOU HAVE THE RIGHT:

To spend time by yourself, with male or female friends, or with your family.

And the most important thing to remember is -- you have the right:

TO END A REALATIONSHIP!

Presidential Proclamation--National Teen Dating Violence Awareness and Prevention Month, 2011

BY THE PRESIDENT OF THE UNITED STATES OF AMERICA

A PROCLAMATION

National Teen Dating Violence Awareness and Prevention Month reflect our Nation's growing understanding that violence within relationships often begins during adolescence. Each year, about one in four teens report being the victim of verbal, physical, emotional, or sexual violence. Abusive relationships can impact adolescent development, and teens that experience-dating violence may suffer long-term negative behavioral and health consequences. Adolescents in controlling or violent relationships may carry these dangerous and unhealthy patterns into future relationships. The time to break the cycle of teen dating violence is now, before another generation falls victim to this tragedy.

Though many communities face the problem of teen dating violence, young people can be afraid to discuss it, or they may not recognize the severity of physical, emotional, or sexual abuse. Parents and other adults can also be uncomfortable acknowledging that young people

experience abuse, or may be unaware of its occurrence. To help stop abuse before it starts, mentors and leaders must stress the importance of mutual respect and challenge representations in popular culture that can lead young people to accept unhealthy behavior in their relationships.

Our efforts to take on teen dating violence must address the social realities of adolescent life today. Technology such as cell phones, email, and social networking websites play a major role in many teenagers' lives, but these tools are sometimes tragically used for control, stalking, and victimization. Emotional abuse using digital technology, including frequent text messages, threatening emails, and the circulation of embarrassing messages or photographs without consent, can be devastating to young teens. I encourage concerned teens, parents, and loved ones to contact The National Teen Dating Abuse Helpline at 1-866- 331-9474 or visit www.LoveIsRespect.org to receive immediate and confidential advice and referrals.

My Administration is committed to engaging a broad spectrum of community partners to curb and prevent teen dating violence. The Department of Justice's Office on Violence Against Women supports collaborative efforts to enhance teens' understanding of healthy relationships, help them identify signs of abuse,

and assist them in locating services. Resources are available at: www.OVW.USDOJ.gov/teen_dating_violence.htm. The Centers for Disease Control and Prevention also provide tools to help prevent dating violence among teens. More information is available at: www.CDC.gov/ChooseRespect.

During National Teen Dating Violence Awareness and Prevention Month -- and throughout the year -- let each of us resolve to do our part to break the silence and create a culture of healthy relationships for all our young people. Adults who respect themselves, their partners, and their neighbors demonstrate positive behaviors to our children -- lessons that will help them lead safe and happy lives free from violence.

NOW, THEREFORE, I, BARACK OBAMA, President of the United States of America, by virtue of the authority vested in me by the Constitution and the laws of the United States, do hereby proclaim February 2011 as National Teen Dating Violence Awareness and Prevention Month. I call upon all Americans to support efforts in their communities and schools, and in their own families, to empower young people to develop healthy relationships throughout their lives and to engage in activities that prevent and respond to teen dating violence.

KESHA STOWE-SPENCE

IN WITNESS WHEREOF, I have hereunto set my hand this thirty-first day of January, in the year of our Lord two thousand eleven, and of the Independence of the United States of America the two hundred and thirty-fifth.

BARACK OBAMA

THE MONTH OF FEBUARY

IS

TEEN DATING VIOLENCE AWARENESS & PREVENTION MONTH

ABOUT THE AUTHOR

Kesha Stowe-Spence the proud Mom of two, Proprietor of STOP Sister Hood Sin Apparel, Author, Founder of The Elizabeth Mae Eaddy Organization, "Free Yourself from Domestic Violence" (www.temeo4dv.org), A certified member of the Domestic Violence Response Team (DVRT), as well as Survivor of Domestic Violence. Kesha is driven to inspire victims of abuse to raise above their circumstances by sharing her own experience of once living the life of a victim of domestic abuses. Kesha was given a second chance May, 2007. God did not add another day to her life because she needed it, he added it because someone out there needed her.

Live the life you were born to live…a life filled with *self love*. ☺

Kesha

www.ingramcontent.com/pod-product-compliance
Lightning Source LLC
Chambersburg PA
CBHW062033040426
42447CB00010B/2265